FUCKING POETRY

peculiar czar

Presentation by *BookLeaf Publishing*

Web: www.bookleafpub.com

E-mail: info@bookleafpub.com

ISBN: 9789357441681

First edition 2023

Established on October 25, 2022. This is mostly about you, for I didn't thought that I would be inspired to write once again, you awakened my sleeping vocabulary. You will never find out but, admiring you was so magical as it was serene.

Somehow, you saved me from times without me asking for it, the compositions that I wrote about you are by far my favourite.

And you are the dearest among all my dandelion wishes, my darling.

ACKNOWLEDGEMENT

Thank you to BookLeaf Publishing for giving me this opportunity to write and express my artistry.

Thank you to Jaycel, my best friend, for being there all the time even though, we are miles apart. I never felt that you were far away, metaphorically and literally, in my heart, my soul sister. Thank you for supporting me ever since we were young with my poetry.

Thank you to Ate Eunice, thank you for reading my compositions and, being there as well even though, you're in a different continent, my legitimate ate from another mother.

To my dandelion wish, thank you for being there, you were the inspiration behind this book. I don't really know why I met you but, it was enchanting and timely.

To Ate Tamerlane, I just want to thank you for listening to my stories and, proofreading my poetry.

To my readers, I express my gratitude to every single one of you and, I hope your appreciate my art.

PREFACE

My thoughts are always racing;
I don't listen to people talking;
but, you have my full attention;

Outside; I'm always reading;
book in hand; story in mind;
but, I'll close the pages for you:

I tend to easily forget;
like where my bloody keys were;
but, I remember little details about you;

the anklet on your right foot;
shallow pulse on your right hand;
the friendship we have;

I guess i'll never understand;
who you are to me;
how rare; for you to be engraved in my memory;

you are not just poetry, you are fucking poetry.

fucking poetry

the last man in my life, called me " fat ";
he waved a bright red flag;
my hopeful hopeless romantic self didn't give
up;
he sang songs of magnificat.

Now however, I want to win in life;
and, he had to exist in this lifetime;
you were an idea in mind;
in this poem; the words are mine;

one day, I'll meet my own pastel blue;
in heartbreaks, they say people are remedies;
if traitors can clone, then darling so can you;

crossing paths with you was not an accident;
you awakened my sleeping vocabulary;
he is full of advices that are prudent;
meeting you was fucking poetry.

I still fucking do

I learned to curse in poems and, in a decade, I
will still fucking do;
I wished on every dandelion I stumbled upon;
feel enchanted when events start to make sense;
and, in the future; I will still fucking do;

I find joy in the smallest things;
I believe that time is a priceless gift;
and, I still fucking do;

I had to grow up fast as a kid,
with that I brought my childish antics;
that way life didn't feel like a battlefield;
and, I still fucking do;

I'm known to be frangible;
and, prone to breakdowns;
I never knew courage;
but, now I fucking do;

and, If I was to marry;
I'll make sure;
till death do us part;
I still fucking do.

fucking art

I fucking left; emotions tainted; blood red;
I've lost all of my confidence;
why does meeting people,
feel like a coincidence?

but, being bilious makes me write;
rib crushing proses; reminds me of the moments;
I cried tears;
like an overflowing faucet;

Then after the storm, came a rainbow;
reflecting colors over my dull window;
I felt sanguine, ready for a new start;
every single thing feels like fucking art.

magical thinking meets fucking reality

manic pixies won't bend their knees; once upon
a time they said " fuck the patriarchy ";
magical thinking meets fucking reality; they
were walking on the sidewalk;
betting on when will the " no entry " sign fall
off;

stepping on brick orange leaves, pointing at
trees;
saying winter is coming; I look at him smiling;
magical thinking meets fucking reality;
I was fighting the winds of destiny;

philosophies clashing; we agree to disagree;
pixie dust fell on the ground;
like the surrender of snow;
my childhood ghost is letting me go;

It was me and my magical thinking;
I felt my hope shrinking,
he spoke words of candour,
him, beautiful mister;

I admired the way he thinks;

I felt smarter after he explains,
surprisingly humorous,
I wore my limitations as armour,

such timely events;
enchantments in instance;
a pleasure;
to meet your acquaintance;

It won't be you and me,
this is just the story;
about how magical thinking;
meets fucking reality.

fucking liberty

cheery, I painted my face,
different colors; everyday;
expressions, I couldn't show it;
for tears meant weakness;

love; I have a lot in me;
like the ashes;
of my failed almosts;

fear; I have a little bit;
I danced frightened;
to the hell of it;

breathing;
darling, I couldn't breathe;
though; it's as natural;
when we bleed;

I seem to always bleed;
my wounds never closed;
traumatic;
since I was a kid;

drama;
people like it;

my family abides;
caged and tied;

unsettling;
poetry are words;
I never spoke;

fight;
I'm the enemy;
without a heart;

stay still;
they maneuver;
I haven't lived;

death;
I'm not scared of death;
but, I can't die yet;

revenge;
bittersweet;
lurking eyes;
all on me;

greedy;
on their knees;
meeting their destiny;

the very moment I gained my fucking liberty.

fucking red

I got fucking mad, I got fucking sad,
everything that he is, is fucking red;
I'm not doing well but, I'm trying my best;
being successful is my biggest revenge;

I bet she rolls her eyes; my admiration fed your
pride;
It was a trap gift wrapped; I was surprised;
bring me the man you showed me;
the one who made me genuinely happy;

I thought you wanted a wife;
but, you wanted the benefits of a friend;
traded a few months for a life;
you made me traumatized;

everything about you is fucking red.

fucking traumatic

Ironic; for a somnolent individual;
fail to slumber;
I felt my chest clench in the middle;
of our family supper;

I only wanted to pour out my love;
Why do I have to suffer?
now I'm composing poems;
like I'm the saddest writer;

but, darling I'm glad that it wasn't meant to be,
being with you;would be the two of us;
digging my own grave of misery;

to me; falling in love has always felt like magic;
I'd do it over and over again;
you destroyed it;
made it fucking traumatic.

a fucking hopeful hopeless romantic

after all the trauma, here I am once again;
watering flowers on the butterfly garden;

making wishes on dandelions;
winter is approaching;
my cheeks are red;
blood is rushing;

the undead emotions live;
poetry books opened;
long stored in the attic;
me; with my crazy antics;

uncontrollable smile;
your gravity drifts;
fixated heart eyes;
I still have it;

the wonders of a fucking hopeful hopeless
romantic.

he fucking will

he told me about the kind of house that he
wanted;
and, I'm pretty sure that he will get it;

I know that he'll propose to his present
girlfriend;
he told me that when you look for a partner;
you should be certain of them;

he is future oriented;
I'm being held hostage by my past;
all my scars opened up;
It's driving me mad;

I'm rooting for you and her;
how perfect it would be;
but, I'm also rooting for you and me;
for I cannot promise;
that it should've been me;

maybe in another universe;
to sugarcoat my belief;
that this world is a curse;
be happy for you;

when you reach;
every single dream;
I will confidently say;
he fucking will.

he fucking told me

he was right; for his age;
he was adequately wise;
But, when I proved him wrong,
in his bittersweet defeat;
he lavishly smiled;

I flicked his forehead;
making him laugh;
are my small wins;

I always believed;
that love is for the brave;
from my hopelessness,
will I be saved?

It's peculiar;
sitting next to my poetry;
he is a walking remote possibility;
befriended me;
with all my temerity;

we cannot speak;
about what's unfinished;
to choose someone;
you have to be sure;

doughty of me;
to wish it was you;
we can never tell;
in full sobriety;

the wisdom;
the certainty;
the look on his face;
he fucking told me.

fucking breathe

paradise island; I wanted to die;
I felt ten hands clasping my neck;
the pressure is too much for a small framed girl;

why can't you be this? why can't you be that?
how can I reach my potential?-
-when I can't even fucking breathe;

today, we're doing the impossible;
everyday, the mountains become smaller;
when I couldn't even grasp-
the ideas of forever from my windows;

all these hurdles are papers rolled in a fish bowl;
some days we're lucky-
some days we're unfortunate-
but, we're always blessed;

-now, we can fucking breathe.

redhill fucking road

a mere stranger; until he became dear to me;
quiet; presence calm, matching what not;
we tend to navigate;
leave the house half past eight;

simple conversation turned into bickering;
friendly encounter; take a second and think;
we've met him before-
we're standing next to poetry;

his fragrance gets stuck in a room like cigarette
smoke-
just like when the wind slaps down in redhill
road-
I accidentally held your wrist;
I couldn't take any risks-

I could only hope that he got used to me;
like how I got used to him;
he'll never experience separation anxiety;
for it will never be the same-

walking on redhill fucking road-
with just your ghost.

fucking childhood

I was alone from seven to seven;
spent nights in a computer shop;
I reminisce and realize;
there was something I can't take back;

I had to grow up really fast;
I can't fail doing simple tasks;
since, I was thirteen-
I'm in a warzone with my own mind.

I want to explore-
but, I have a reputation to uphold;

every choice I make must profit with gold;
all I know are things that I should;
It's not my parents fault;
that I couldn't redeem my fucking childhood.

a fucking dandelion

three wishes; one of them is you;
I'm the opposite of simple-
what's simple is you;
maybe, I have a sight for things-
that are beautiful;

and, if he was a flower;
he was a fucking dandelion;
solitary with a thousand possibilities;
he makes your wishes come true-

they say it's color reflects the sun;
he's not mine but, I made him infinite;
he'll be the last to know;
in flowery words; he will everglow;

and, he was also soft yellow;
he radiates serenity and joy;
once the wind struck; he gracefully flew-
people like him; come in a few.

my fucking poetry

In a place of solitude; only you and me,
in a crowd of blurred alien faces;
you, with your back turned;
I know those shoulders from anywhere;

with a distance so great; a world so small;
my confession in paper airplanes;
oh darling, if it ever reaches you;
hear my love above all the white noise;

my poetry was standing next to me;
quietly; not saying a word;
when he speaks; he opens galaxies;
impactful; he jumped out from piano keys;

in an auditorium, empty seats;
I was the only audience;
I admired him-
-though my poetry doesn't recognize me;

my poetry will never know;
he was translated into a prose;
the person who admires him-
is as fragile as a rose;

as soft as wishing on flowers;
petals fleeting as tiny whispers-
you are artwork; a masterpiece;
you're not mine; but, I own the words-

my fucking poetry.

fucking magical

handwritten by a wine drunk woman,
God sure made you well;
allowing me to meet you-
was it bizarre to meet someone wantonly?-

we all know that you're not the one for me,
but, I guess we leave a space in our railway life;
just like the seat next to mine-
you can come back whenever you like;

so hopeful, wishful that you'll never leave;
a lachrymose of a story;
he was solace to my anxiety;
a millpond to my tsunami-

Isn't it a pity? for all I can do is live in the
moment;
write poetry and wish for the best;
a ghost of a chance; a riskful dance;
I thought I won't feel this way again;

but, every time I fall in love;
it feels so fucking magical.

fucking horror

It's been ten days since the day he left;
somehow, there's a lilac nymph floating;
she's in the enchanted forest in my chest;
wondering where her normie friend went;

I'm in an old theatre; heart in hand-
-poems in the other; reciting without a
microphone;
he was standing there; unable to understand;
crickets sounds whilst the doves have flown;

the seasons are changing; I'm still writing;
my vocabulary was sleeping;
you've awakened the dull library;
what am I going to do with my nymph?

you turned into a poltergeist;
you're alive but, somehow died;
I'm mourning over the living;
you haunt all the settings;

you're a nuisance in the corridors;
I still see you where you used to be;
you scare me, though you're a normie;
for I never felt lonely-

and, being lonesome is a fucking horror.

I fucking hope that it's you

every song I whisper, it all means so true;
heaven is real, from all the pictures drawn;
my manic self wrote and painted until the dawn;
my poetry are songs unsung;

my poetry translates my misery;
he said it wouldn't complete me;
somehow I am certain;
someone out there is walking-
in restless shoes;

I'm pretty sure it's magic;
for things that cannot be seen;
tends to last forever;
but, love and sadness are both intangible;

it wasn't entirely hell;
for my butterfly wings didn't burn;
but, I would burn for someone;
staying for every season that ends-

whoever you may be;
I hope that you'll hold my asthmatic hands,
calm my wrathful heart;
appreciate my peculiar art;

feel the blaze of my love;
the coldness of my touch;
feel the passion in my poetry;
the comfort in my songs;

that wherever you are;
you'd carry a piece of me;
that I'm more of your friend-
than your lover;

that I'd meet him in my prime;
be my partner in crime;
silence my chaos and,
my vengeful spirit;

they say my standard cuts to a few;
I beg to differ-
I just want to marry my bestfriend;
and, I fucking hope that it's you.

so fucking absent minded

I easily forget, I'm absent minded;
but, I remember the day I met you;
at the airport, Nelson Road, Heathrow;
you asked if we're at north tees too;

I easily forget, I'm absent minded;
but, I remember the first night;
we became housemates;
I stored the leftovers and,
you washed the dishes;

I easily forget, I'm absent minded;
but, I remember when you asked me;
if I could keep your notes;
I went on a trip; you asked if when will I be
home;

I easily forget, I'm absent minded;
but, I remember the first bus ride;
somehow, the seat next to mine;
was always yours;

I easily forget, I'm absent minded;
but, I remember orientation day;
we don't speak much but,

we noticed that we both play tricks on our pens;

I easily forget, I'm absent minded;
but, I remember the first walk home;
it became my favourite thing after bus rides;

I easily forget, I'm absent minded,
but, I remember the moments;
that we shared in the kitchen;
it was the first time I cooked for my crush;

I easily forget, I'm absent minded,
but, I remember every class and practice
sessions;
you pay attention to detail;
we both expected to fail;

I easily forget, I'm absent minded;
but, I remember realizing-
that you fit in my present timeline;
with me, anticipating your departure;

I easily forget, I'm absent minded;
but, I get flashbacks of your vivid face;
smiling, with your eyes fixated on me;
pearl earrings, brown corduroy dress;

I easily forget, I'm absent minded;
but, I remember you asking if I was home safe;

how, we learned to agree to disagree;
you're savant, the learnings you told me;

I easily forget, I'm so fucking absent minded;
but, I'll remember you forever;
probably, in such time until I get alzheimer's-
a reference that only you'll understand.

I can fucking wait forever

he put his glasses on, as I took off mine;
maybe, love does has a thing with time;
his hot coffee first thing in the morning;
my venti iced latte through the night;

the documentaries that he watches;
the books that I read as sedatives;
he writes in his journal, as I turn him into
poems;
his bullet planner empty, mine full of plans;

bewildered with how violet I can be;
he said purple, more vibrant-
than the lilac I have in hand;
I smiled, he's specific in detail-

I'm specific in art-
though, I'm not so good at my talent;
I try to rhyme him; he said I walked too fast;
he doesn't like talking too much;

he is my best friend-
regardless of my religion;
we were oceans apart;
now, we're in the same region;

I'll recite this poem one day;
unknowingly, under the rainy sky I visioned-
it will be the best gloom of my life-

He asked " have we met before? "
I said " never ";
but, I've known you forever;
lucky you, I can fucking wait forever.

the fucking farewell

it was the third of january;
I didn't know what's coming for me;
that day he was so cheery;
he has some news to break in;

my mood was as bright;
as the hot pink in my hair;
I flicked his forehead;
after winning a bet that's fair;

I was so happy to see him;
he was so jovial to leave;
he said " see you around "
but, when will that be?

I showed him that I wasn't sad;
but, my heart felt like an abyss;
my enthusiasm is a facade;
he was filled with fucking bliss;

out of all the people;
you were my favourite;
and, I don't like people;
you certainly know it;

I'll keep your friendship;
just as you should mine;
and if you ask me;
I'll say that I'm fine;

he had to wait for me;
at the fucking junction;
negative three degrees;
I endured the cold;

problems don't get fixed;
with a bottle of wine;
you're not coming back;
if it's not in the timeline;

my walk from home;
I will never forget it;
a thousand whys;
it felt like a thousand miles;

every damn song hits hard;
make me feel unwell;
it's time to move forward;
after the fucking farewell.

9 789357 441681